dabble lab

CREATE CRAZY STOP-MOTION VIDEOS

Thomas Kingsley Troupe

raintree
a Capstone company — publishers for children

Raintree is an imprint of Capstone Global Library Limited, a company incorporated in England and Wales having its registered office at 264 Banbury Road, Oxford, OX2 7DY – Registered company number: 6695582

www.raintree.co.uk
myorders@raintree.co.uk

Edited by Shelly Lyons
Designed by Sarah Bennett
Original illustrations © Capstone Global Library Limited 2020
Picture research by Morgan Walters
Production by Katy LaVigne
Originated by Capstone Global Library Ltd
Printed and bound in India

978 1 4747 8736 9 (hardback)
978 1 4747 6796 5 (paperback)

British Library Cataloguing in Publication Data
A full catalogue record for this book is available from the British Library.

Acknowledgements
We would like to thank the following for permission to reproduce photographs: All photos shot by Capstone Studio, Karon Dubke, with the exception of these: Shutterstock: Astarina, (hand) design element; Becris, (film) design element throughout; Can Yesil, (phone); Darcraft, design element throughout; Dzmltry, background 14; Fer Gregory, bottom right 15; Lightspring, background 45; Natasha Pankina, design element throughout; ONYXprj, (laptop) bottom right 44; Seth Gallmeyer, (notebook) design element throughout; Shorena Tedliashvili, (filmstrip) design element throughout; silm, (filmstrip) design element throughout; vector illustration, design element throughout; Vissay, (poster) bottom 45; Vyacheslav Sakhatsky, 7

Every effort has been made to contact copyright holders of material reproduced in this book. Any omissions will be rectified in subsequent printings if notice is given to the publisher.

All the internet addresses (URLs) given in this book were valid at the time of going to press. However, due to the dynamic nature of the internet, some addresses may have changed, or sites may have changed or ceased to exist since publication. While the author and publisher regret any inconvenience this may cause readers, no responsibility for any such changes can be accepted by either the author or the publisher.

CONTENTS

Movie magic

An action figure walks across a scene and stops to do a backflip. A little horse made of clay gallops and jumps over a fence. Is this some sort of magic? No, it's stop-motion animation!

Stop-motion is an animation technique that uses objects and photography rather than drawings. It is created one frame at a time. A person takes a photo of an object and then moves the object slightly before the next photo is snapped. When the images are played back in a rapid sequence, the object appears to move on its own.

Stop-motion success guide

Be patient Making a stop-motion video can be a time-consuming and sometimes frustrating project. With practice and patience, you'll make your vision come to life.

Keep it simple It's easy to imagine a blockbuster video, but that's hard to achieve. Start with an easy, short video to gain some stop-motion experience.

Experiment Though you'll quickly learn the basics, don't be afraid to try new things. Keep your video fresh and exciting to make it stand out.

What you'll need:

☆ an idea
☆ a script
☆ a storyboard
☆ characters
☆ a phone, digital or tablet camera
☆ a location or background
☆ lights or lamps
☆ a microphone
☆ editing software

Making a stop-motion video shouldn't cost much. Most of what you'll need can be found around your home. Some of the best stop-motion videos out there are the ones made with no budget.

Camera ready

One of the most important elements in making your video will be your camera. Find a digital camera that is simple to use and able to take one photo at a time. As most stop-motion videos are 8 fps (frames per second) to 10 fps, that means you'll need to take 8 to 10 pictures to make 1 second of video!

Phone cameras

If you're able to use a smartphone as your camera, you're in luck. Not only are phone cameras easy to use, many of them can use stop-motion video apps. Always ask an adult for permission to download an app. Make sure you clear plenty of space in the phone's memory. Remember, you'll be taking hundreds of photos.

Tablet cameras

Using a tablet such as an iPad is a good option. Like a smartphone, a tablet will be able to use stop-motion apps, which will make shooting and editing easier. But some tablets are bulky and can be hard to keep steady when each photo is taken.

PRO TIP

There are lots of free stop-motion apps to choose from. Free apps may have limited features, but for a beginner video-maker, they can do the trick.

Digital cameras

Another option for capturing stop-motion is a digital camera. Just make sure there's a memory card with enough room on it to hold a lot of pictures. One disadvantage to using digital cameras is that they don't have built-in stop-motion apps.

Tripods

No matter what camera you use, find a way to lock it into place. Using a tripod is a great option. The less your camera moves with each photo taken, the better your results.

Use a tripod to lock your camera into place.

Types of tripods
- ☆ standard (for shooting straight on)
- ☆ top-down (for shooting from above)
- ☆ smartphone (have a grip to hold smartphone in place)
- ☆ tablet (have a mount for stability)

Casting call

Every good film starts with a good idea and great characters. Look around you. There are thousands of things lying around your house that could star in your next film.

Your favourite teddy bear and your little brother's best action toy could meet for an ice cream. Two toy cars could race against time – and each other. A clay monster could pick flowers from a garden. The ideas are as endless as your imagination, so give your imagination a workout!

Action figures

One of the most important elements of your video will be the characters. Find objects that lend themselves to action. Poseable action figures work well. But just like real actors, some toys are better than others.

If your script calls for a lot of movement and different poses, look for toys that can bend at the elbows, knees, hips and other joints.

PRO TIP

Unless you're shooting from above, make sure you test your figures to ensure they can stand up on their own. A toy that keeps falling over will make your video a lot harder to shoot!

Change it up!

If you'd like your characters to be able to show emotions, make sure you use fun characters that have expressions you can change. If you can't find any, make your own creatures. Monsters with changeable eyes and mouths work well. In one shot, a monster can wink. In the next shot, she can have wide-open eyes and an open mouth. Think of all the expressions you can make!

PRO TIP

Use felt or paper to create several different eyes and mouths for your characters. Be silly and have fun with it!

☺ 😄 ☹ 😋 😐 😆 😖

If you've got some thick card and scissors, consider creating cut-out characters. You can form animals, robots and even monsters.

You can cut out or draw different facial expressions to bring them to life.

Use fasteners to attach arms and legs that can move.

If you decide to make paper characters, it will be best to shoot from above.

PRO TIP

These owls make fun characters. Make your own from cardboard tubes and coloured paper and card!

Dolls

If you'd like your character to look a little bit more realistic – try using dolls. They can look sweet or creepy, depending on how you film them. While they might not stand up as well as action figures, some dolls come with stands to hold them in place.

Everyday objects

Want to do something different?
Try using everyday objects as characters.

☆ A pencil can be positioned differently in each
   shot of your video. It will appear to be moving
   around on its own.

☆ Draw on a whiteboard or
   chalkboard. For each shot,
   redraw the parts you
   want to move.

☆ Place sticky notes in a design.
   Move them around a bit for
   each shot. The notes will look
   like they move on their own.

☆ Or ask a patient friend or family
   member to pose, one move at a time,
   one shot at a time.

Redraw the parts you want to move.

(Just make sure you completely erase the parts you don't want to see in the next shots.)

Script-tastic

Once you have finalised your idea and your characters, it's best to write a script. Even if none of the characters will talk, a script can help you stick to your story. Like an outline, a script can be a good guide to make sure you don't forget anything.

It's not important to make your script look like a REAL film script. You just need to write down the location of the scene, which characters are there, and what they're doing. If your characters will talk, write down what they're going to say. This is called dialogue.

script ☺

Well, hello there, Marvin.

Mighty fine day for a walk, isn't it?

SCRIPT

The <u>scene</u> tells us where the video shoot will take place.

Outdoors – bright, sunny afternoon

<u>Action</u> tells us what the characters will do.

The owls move towards each other. In the background we see some clouds and trees.

<u>Dialogue</u> tells us what the characters will say.

Harry (raising an eyebrow and tilting his head): "Well, hello there, Marvin. Mighty fine day for a walk, isn't it?"

shot #1

shot #2

shot #5

shot #6

SCRIPT

Outdoors — bright, sunny afternoon

The owls move towards each other. In the background
we see some clouds and trees.

Harry (raising an eyebrow and tilting his head): "Well,
hello there, Marvin. Mighty fine day for a walk, isn't it?"

Marvin (bowing his head a bit): "Yes it is, Harry. I've got
a joke for you. Wanna hear it?"

shot #3

shot #4

shot #7

shot #8 — That makes one second of a video!

One thing to remember when writing a script: The longer the script, the longer the video will be. Remember, each tiny movement your character makes will be one frame. If a one-page script takes you six hours to film, imagine how long it would take to shoot a 30-page script!

PRO TIP

Keep your first few stop-motion scripts short — perhaps one to two pages long. Once you see how long it takes to shoot that, you'll have an idea of how much work it takes to make a longer video.

Storyboard basics

A good companion piece to your script is a storyboard. A storyboard is like a series of comic book panels. Each panel is a scene that you draw. For stop-motion, each scene is a movement the character makes. Is Bill the Alligator going to turn his head? Draw it!

The scenes are arranged in the order you want them to appear in the video. A storyboard will help you keep your characters' movements in the right order as you shoot the video.

scene #1

A sunny day in the woods

scene #2

Owls enter from opposite ends of the screen.

scene #3

They walk towards each other.

"Well, hello there, Marvin. Mighty fine day for a walk, isn't it?"

scene #4

They meet in the middle.

"Yes it is, Harry."

scene #5

scene #6

Don't worry, your storyboard doesn't have to be perfect. Stick figures will do. If you can tell which character is which and what they're doing, that's all you need. Having both a script and a storyboard might seem like too much, but the more you plan your video, the better it'll be.

Prepping for the shoot

Location

Finding the best location for your video is extremely important. Once you have all of your equipment together, you can set everything up.

Find a place that's out of the way and near a plug socket. Because stop-motion can take time to film, try to keep everything set up until you've finished.

Good ideas
☆ spare bedroom
☆ quiet corner
☆ playroom

Bad ideas
☆ kitchen table
☆ bathroom
☆ hallway

Background

Think about where your video is going to take place. Is it a city street? A lush, green countryside? Maybe inside your character's home? To bring the scene to life, it's good to have a background.

Background options: Draw your own background, build a set using click-together bricks or building toys, print out a scenic picture or don't use background at all. Remember to consider the size of your characters. If you're using big characters, go with a large background.

If you'd like a variety of backgrounds, try using a green screen. Just shoot your photos against a lime-green background. When you've finished, you can use a program or app to substitute the green for any sort of background you want.

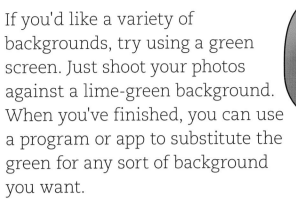

PRO TIP

Are you trying out a green screen? Make sure your characters aren't wearing a colour that's too close to the green screen's colour. Their body parts could disappear when you add the background.

Those trees look so real!

They're not real?

Lighting

Stop-motion can take time to film, so it's important to light your set or background. Using a lamp or two to brighten up the space is an easy solution. Just position them out of your shots, turn them on, and keep them there.

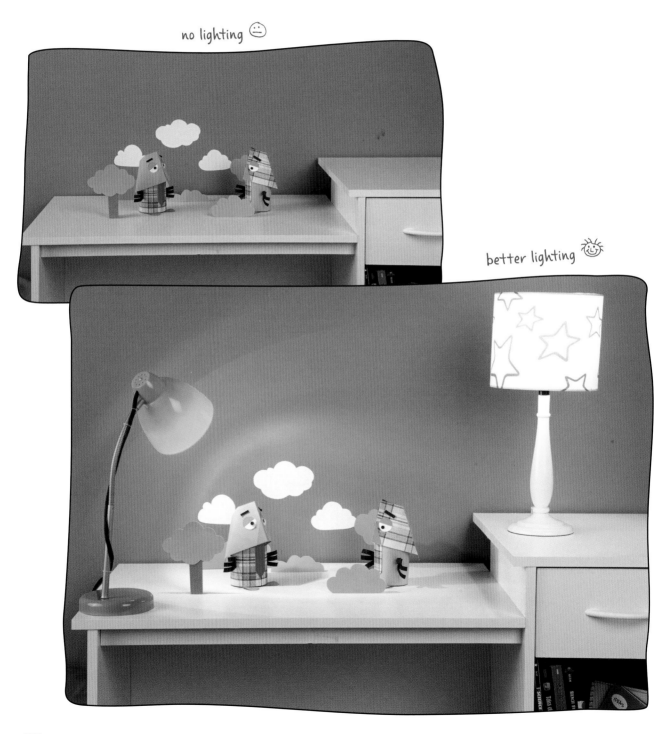

no lighting 😐

better lighting 😄

As nice as natural light from a window can look, it's not dependable. Because the sun moves throughout the day, the lighting in your video will change. The shadows your characters create will move and become distracting.

The sun moves too much to be a reliable source of lighting.

PRO TIP

Torches aren't good for adding light to a video. Not only do they provide a limited amount of light, they depend on batteries that can die. Lamps or ceiling lights are your best bet.

poor lighting ☹

Action!

Shooting

You've done all of your prep work, now it's time to shoot the video. When shooting your video, remember to refer to your storyboard and script. They will tell you the order of your shots and scenes. Position your character or object the way you want it to appear. This will be picture number one in a long series of shots.

Once your character is in place, position your camera. Make sure everything you want to see is in the frame. When you like the way the scene looks, lock your camera into place on a tripod.

Take your first picture! Work out your character's next move and position it. It's best to make the movements very small for each image. The smaller the movement, the smoother the action will look when it's finished.

Take the second picture, reposition your character or object, and take the next picture. Repeat this over and over until you've finished your scene. Don't be afraid to look at what you've shot to make sure you like the way it's turning out. Repeat this over and over until you've taken all of the shots for the scene.

Remember, stop-motion means taking A LOT of photos. If you're satisfied, start the next scene. It's OK to take breaks between scenes, too. When you've reached the end of your script and storyboard, you've finished shooting.

Step 1: Take your first picture.

PRO TIP

Make sure your hands don't show up in the photos. Seeing hands in the video will ruin the illusion of stop-motion. If it does happen, just delete that shot and take it again.

That's a wrap!

Step 2: Move your character a tiny bit.

Step 3: Take another picture.

Step 4: Make another small movement.

Step 5: Take another picture, and repeat!

Uploading photos

If you're using an app designed for making stop-motion videos, you probably won't need to import the photos. If you're using a digital camera, you'll need to get the photos onto a computer. Connect the camera and find the file folder on your computer. Copy all of the images you took and drop them into a folder.

Open the software you plan to use to assemble and edit your video. Highlight all of the photos you've just taken and drag them into the program. You should see them pop into the video line of your editing software.

There are a lot of photos, Harry.

Yes, lots of photos, Marvin.

Cutting room

Editing

Now comes the exciting part! You'll be able to play a rough cut of your video. Press "play" on the program or app and watch your hard work come to life. Don't forget that the video will still need a bit of fine-tuning.

Watch the video a few times. Does it move too slowly? If so, you can adjust the fps (frames per second) of the video. It's usually best to set this to 8 fps or 10 fps. Also, keep an eye out for frames that might have an accidental hand or finger in them. If you spot one, delete it.

Finishing touches

Adding dialogue/narration

As of now, you've made a silent stop-motion video. But what if you wrote dialogue or want a narrator to explain what's happening? In that case, you'll need to record the voices that will accompany the video. Most apps have an option to add audio to the video.

Adding music

Have you ever tried to watch a film without music or a soundtrack? Music can completely change the mood and feel of a video. Try adding a little bit of music to your video to see how different it feels.

PRO TIP

Try making your own music to add to the video. If you want to use someone else's music, ask for permission first. If you use someone's music without permission, you may have to pay a fine.

Visual effects

Some stop-motion and video apps have options to change the colour of your film. If you'd like your animation to look like an old-fashioned film, try black and white. For a futuristic look, try using a negative filter. This filter inverts the colour.

Sound effects

Adding sound effects can take your video to the next level. If your video features a character who tells a joke, add a cymbal sound at the end of the joke. Small sound effects can make a big difference!

Title

To give your short film a proper look and feel, add a title. The title can come in over the action, over a freeze-frame or on a separate shot completely. While most apps have a built-in title generator, you could also consider making your own.

End credits

Give credit where credit is due. If you had some help with the filming or the ideas, make sure you add the people from your crew to the credits. As with the titles, this can be done in a number of ways. Some apps make it easy to add credits. If not, you can create credits using some of your newly learned stop-motion techniques.

The **BIG** premiere

Sharing your video

Now that you've finished your animation, you'll want to share it with your soon-to-be fans. Make a big deal about it! You put a lot of hard work into this. Have a premiere night at your house and invite your family to watch it. If your friends have made some videos too, turn it into a film festival! Want to see if people around the world will watch it? Ask your parents/guardians to help you upload it to the internet (YouTube, Vimeo).

That's a wrap!

Now that you've created your first stop-motion animation, go and make another one! Using what you've learned, you can make something even better than your original. With a little time, practice and imagination, your next stop-motion video will make your friends and family "stop" their own "motion" to watch!

PRO TIP

If you don't want to use your real name (or other identifying information), make sure you remove it from the video before posting it online.

Meet your film instructor

Thomas Kingsley Troupe is an amateur filmmaker who has been making films and videos since he was at secondary school. Thomas has worked in the visual effects department for a handful of Hollywood films and shows. He has also written and directed a number of short films for the 48 Hour Film Fest & Z Fest contests and loves creating funny videos with his own sons at home. Thomas says, "Making films is the BEST. It can be a lot of work, but finishing a film to show to your friends and family is WORTH IT!"

Find out more

Books

Animation and Presentation from Scratch (Code it Yourself), Rachel Ziter (Raintree, 2018)

Cracking Animation: The Aardman Book of 3D Animation, Peter Lord (Thames and Hudson, 2016)

Website

bbc.co.uk/cbbc/watch/p02hw9t0
Watch a video of someone creating a stop-motion animation, and learn simple techniques to improve your films.

Glossary

animation activity of making films using drawings, pictures or computer graphics

app computer application

audio sound, especially the sound portion of a film or TV programme

dialogue words spoken between two or more characters; in writing, dialogue is set between speech marks

edit cut and rearrange pieces of film to make a film or TV programme

freeze-frame frame of a motion-picture film that is repeated to give the illusion of a static picture

green screen technique of photographing or filming an actor or object against a green backdrop and replacing the backdrop with material from a different image using a colour filter

negative filter filter that inverts the colour of your photo

scene part of a story, play or film that shows what is happening in one place and time

script written down story of a play, film or TV programme

soundtrack recording of music from a film or play

stop-motion animation technique in which an object is moved a little in each shot, and then all shots are put together to make a continuous film

storyboard series of drawings that shows the plot of a TV programme or film

technique method or way of doing something that requires skill

Apps and software

Green Screen, by Do Ink – helps users create videos using the green screen effect

iMovie, by Apple – app to create your own films

Movie Maker 10, by Microsoft – full filmmaking software for all budding artists

Stop Motion Studio, by CATEATER, LLC – app that walks users through the entire process of making a stop-motion film

Index